Anatomy of a
VOLUME
PROFILE
TRADER

By Bruce Levy
FuturesTradeRoom.com

THE HIDDEN PLAYBOOK
FOR GROWING YOUR ACCOUNT

TABLE OF CONTENTS

Introduction

Anatomy of a Volume Profile Trader was written for those who want to trade for a living. Most beginning traders believe that the ability to capture tops and bottoms along with never losing is what it takes to make it in trading. While this may occasionally happen, it is very far from the truth and is not necessary. This book attempts to increase entry, exit and open order handling efficiency through advanced methods of Volume Profile Analysis. Both Retail Speculators and Professional Money Managers can use these methods to sharpen their overall directional trading in any market or time-frame. By applying Volume Profile Analysis, the trader adds a statistical edge to their trading right away.

To get the best results out of this material be sure to review your charts as you pick up new concepts; this will help to solidify the information so that the patterns begin to stand out for you. In addition, you may take a short quiz available at the end of each section before moving on.

The Volume Profile Indicator has allowed me the ability to immediately read the current state of the market with absolute accuracy. This is because when market participants have committed capital through buying and selling it leaves a pattern in the form of a bell curve. This lets the trader predict the future development of price in this area based on certain patterns found in the bell curve which is covered in detail later in this book. Understanding how price reacts to certain levels and knowing what strategies to use is an invaluable asset when it comes to formulating   trade   ideas.

Over the years I've developed a method of trading these patterns, Volume Profile Trading Secrets, which I will share with you. The trading levels found in the profile provide valuable insight into the order-structure and psychology of the market. The levels give me a general idea of what the market wants to do so I can confirm my trade ideas before committing capital.

Before we get into the details of I want to emphasize the importance of manual back testing. To get the most out of this book you'll want to spend time sim trading in market replay, as well as manually back-testing bar by bar. The amount of information you retain from reading is said to be as little as 10% if you were to just read a book and put it down without applying the knowledge. However, if you take action by analyzing your charts with these methods your retention rate goes up to about 90%, it becomes ingrained in your memory through the kinesthetic action. If you want to be able to pick up on specific patterns that pop out of a chart you must become proficient in back-testing. This will allow you to train your reticular activating system (RAS) to search for these patterns and to know how to differentiate between successful and unsuccessful variations. Knowing how to identify the difference between a high probability pattern, and one that is similar, but likely to fail, is a key distinction in the success of a trader. By the end of this book you'll start to understand that the charts are indeed a story of traders hopes and dreams, an aggregation of mass psychology, one with predictable patterns of human behavior. The aim for this book is to give you the base foundation to identify high probability trade setups using the volume profile to exploit these repeating patterns in real-time.

SECTION ONE:

VOLUME AND PROFILE

Chapter 1

CLASSICAL VOLUME

Volume traded at price is the most important aspect of volume profile trading. It is the foundation for which all trading decisions are made. As prices fluctuate it leaves a trail, and like a shrewd detective we gather the evidence and analyze it for clues. In this case the evidence is the amount of volume traded at price. This volume figure shows us how much, or how little interest each price level holds. In order to execute a trade the evidence should be distinct and meaningful, not vague and general. Volume traded affects the movement of price because when there is higher volume at price, there is also a larger amount of existing transactions which must be cleared before moving on.

When a trade is taken in the futures markets it is matched to an opposite trade; a buyer is matched to a seller. When this occurs, the quantity traded is available for viewing as it is added to volume at price. The volume trader attempts to analyze this data in ways that are useful to making an informed trading decision.

The 2 basic tenets of the Volume Profile are: high volume at price indicates high participation, low volume at price indicates low participation. High volume = lower ATR (average true range), or lower volatility, and thus slower acceleration of price through the y-axis. Low Volume = higher ATR potential, or higher volatility and faster price movement potential. By utilizing such volume at price analysis, we can distinguish between areas of support, resistance, range bound trading and price continuation zones which will be covered in later sections.

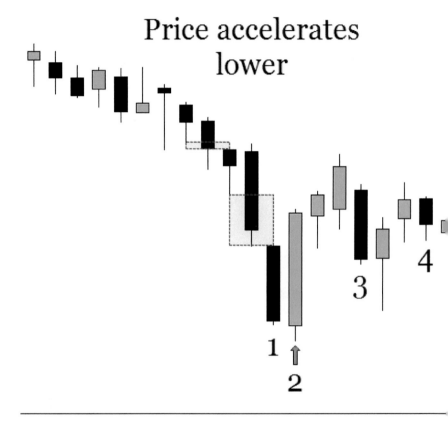

Price accelerates lower

1
2
3
4

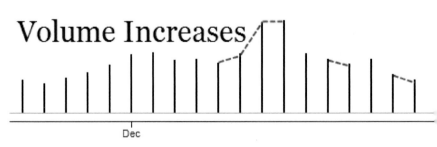

Volume Increases

Dec

1.1 Basic volume indicator

Diagram 1.1 shows a classical volume indicator in the lower panel. As price accelerates lower the buyers demand more of the available supply and the volume increases as buyers are being built into bar 1. In bar 2 it closes strong on the highs, the buyer's started to accumulate in bar 1 and it became apparent that the buyers were in control by bar 2 now that it has closed greater than bar 2.

Next, price continues to trade sideways in a range. The down bars (3 and 4) show a decline in volume, or a lack of selling interest. This method of technical analysis is referred to as the VSA (Volume Spread Analysis) and can be quite useful when you're looking to time an entry.

This is how typical volume is read. In this book we will turn volume on its side (literally) to see volume traded at price which will give us a new perspective for which to base our trade decisions.

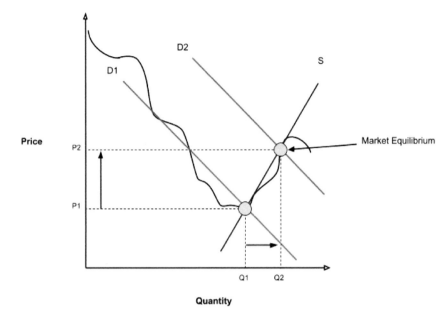

1.2 Line chart depicted over a supply and demand curve.

Changes in trend show areas of short-term market equilibrium, or pauses prior to a change in direction. At D1, buyers come in, at D2 the last buyer buys and supply overpowers the market. A retest of these areas will result in a future reaction in price.

The above diagram shows a supply and demand curve which is applicable to any auction market such as the Futures markets. The volume traded at these turning points often leaves imbalances as many traders selling short into the prior downtrend are now trapped. As price returns to these levels they look to offset their losing positions near break-even. A build-out in the profile (which we will get to later) will show us where these orders are clustered. It is at these equilibrium points that price makes support and resistance in the future. These hidden areas cannot be seen in a classical volume indicator. The volume profile indicator attempts to record such levels through tick by tick updating of all orders at price.

The concept of volume traded at price is easy to grasp; for each price level, there is a corresponding number of contracts which have been traded at that price. The profile simply logs that data and represents it as a horizontal graphic on the chart.
Note the highlighted trading range, this represents a bell curve distribution. Traders take this value area into consideration because it represents liquidity.

Price	Volume
50.85	5
50.84	23
50.83	456 < Value Area High (VAH)
50.82	984
50.81	1597
50.80	**4674 < Point of Control (POC)**
50.79	3522
50.78	1422
50.77	122 < Value Area Low (VAL)
50.76	56
50.75	52
50.74	22
50.73	9
50.72	3
50.71	1

If price were to trade above, or below the value area high, or low we would be expecting responsive activity to push price back into the trading range between the VAH and VAL.

If however price is able to be traded above or below the value area for a sustained period of time we could expect initiative trading activity to push price away from the area and away from the POC.

Q. Volume at Price logs what data?

A. Executed orders at the bid or ask.

Chapter #2

TIME VALUE

Time Value

If you spend time with someone, there is a chance that they add value to your life; if they don't that's something re-consider. The markets work in a similar fashion. As trader's trade within a range for an extended period that level begins to build value. As the number of contracts increases at the current price, so does the relative value of that trade level. It represents the fair value of current market conditions. If traders bring the price down too far and buyers come in for a bargain, this is called an unfair value area low (VAL). If on the other hand traders bring price up too high and cause sellers to step in, this area would be known as the unfair value area high (VAH). The point at which the most amount of trading takes place holds the control of the market, causing price to return to it when going to unfair levels. This high value area acts as a general magnet for price and most of the trading is done at this level. In biology, we know all organisms seek equilibrium, in the markets we consider equilibrium to be the Point of Control (POC). The POC is the price level with the most amount of contracts traded.

Equilibrium can be defined as: "The condition in which all acting influences are balanced or canceled by equal opposing forces, resulting in a stable system."

The influence of buyers and sellers are essentially equal, causing price to trade within the point of control. However, traders can move price outside of a value area into unfair value areas, when price spends a substantial amount of time in these unfair value areas it begins to build new value and begins to trend in that direction, seeking new unfair highs and unfair lows. This process of development and distribution repeats itself on every time-frame.

If price spends 2 TPO's (Time Price Opportunity) or 60 minutes outside of the value area we would consider price to be finding new value. This work is based on Peter J. Steidlemayers Market Profile Handbook. However, in my experience I have found this 2 TPO count to be somewhat arbitrary in a 24-hour market. I prefer to look at this 2 TPO print as an <u>alert</u> to *bring my attention to the volume traded in those areas outside the value area.* I look to see if the profile is building as price is staying outside of that value area. If it is then there is a good chance the 2 TPO print will hold and price will eventually continue in that direction. Any retests of the prior trading range should be met with rejection if price has traded enough volume in the new 2 TPO zone. For example, if we look at a candlestick we could consider the area between the open and the close to contain the highest value trading range. The wicks of the candle would be considered unfair value areas, so a retest of the open or close after 2 TPO's outside of the range should serve as a rejection area. In later sections, we will discuss the standard deviations of such value areas and breakdown the trading range.

Q. What is the POC?

A. The POC is the Point of Control, it is the price level with the most number of contracts traded.

Chapter 3

VOLUME PROFILE

Volume Profile

Volume profile is a tool for which no trader should be without. Its uses for identifying opportunities are extensive, and the profile is unique in that it does not necessarily clutter a chart in the way conventional indicators would. The profile gives the trader a map for which you can look to for guidance. The volume profile plots volume traded at price, the point of control, the value area low, and the value area high; all important trade reference points.

The value area highs and the value area lows are separated into standard deviations. The main value area fits within one standard deviation (68%) of the profile. The unfair value areas fall within the 2nd standard deviations (95%) and the third standard deviation covering 99.7%. It is between the second and third standard deviation that we expect price to quickly rebound and return to the value area. If price builds value outside the third standard deviation zone we call this initiative trading and expect a new trend to take place.

Q. What should you look for in the 2-3 std. dev. range when price is attempting to move into a new area?

A. Development of at least 2 TPO's (acts as initial alert). Also, above average volume traded outside this area is confirmation that value is being accepted. A lack of volume indicates declining interest in that direction.

If price trades in the third standard deviation zone and quickly returns to value we would call this responsive activity. These concepts of initiative and responsive trading were created by Steidlmayer and allow us to standardize how we communicate about the markets activity. When combined with classical technical analysis, order flow, price action patterns or any other methods of analysis the trader exponentially increases their chances of success.

3.1 Point of Control and Profile

In 3.1 the profile on the right shows a yellow point of control.

As traders built this value area over 3-4 days the range became oversaturated. This means that all the trading that needed to be done at this level was mostly finished. A low volume day along with a break of the lows of the range created the overheard resistance needed to push price through the low volume area near 48.

Your profile indicator should show information for whatever is showing on your screen. This is called MAP display, or dynamic display. In addition, your profile should be set to CalculateOnBarClose = false; so that you can see the volume being built as the orders come into the market.

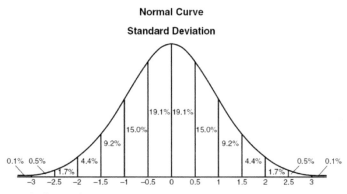

Normal Curve

Standard Deviation

3.2 Normal distribution
The Normal Distribution we use for trading the profile identifies a standard deviation range from 1-3 standard deviations (sigmas).

I have personally found that expanding the value areas to 2 sigma affords me the most realistic boundaries when looking for responsive activity. The market's volatility is usually overstated and so sharp moves outside the 1 sigma range is normal as retail traders pile in every time the market appears to pick a direction. I also consider a test of the 3rd sigma to be the maximum extension in a responsive market.

A responsive market is the opposite of an initiative market where traders essentially buy a breakout and price continues. A responsive market is mean reverting, meaning that once price trades outside the normal range it will reverse and come back into the middle of the trading range.

Q. What is responsive activity?

A. Responsive trading activity is similar to mean reversion activity in a price range. Price will reverse at the value areas thus creating responsive activity.

Q. What do you look for when analyzing Responsive Activity in the 2-3 Std. Dev. range?

A.   *Any tests of the 2-3 std. dev. area should be under 2TPO's (60Minutes) and include lower overall volume development indicating a lack of interest*

Chapter 4:

TYPES OF PROFILES

Types of Profiles

There are three types of profiles:
1. Blocked (Playtykurtic)
2. Normal Distribution (Mesokurtic)
3. Elongated (Leptokurtic)

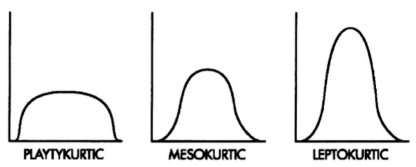

4.1 Three main types of profiles.
The normal distribution (Mesokurtic) represents an idealized finished profile. The elongated profile (Leptokurtic) represents the overly built profile awaiting distribution into new value areas; this means a breakout is imminent. The blocked profile (Playtkurtic) represents continuation trading, or a search for new value; price is not spending much time in any one area and value has not been found yet. During this stage volatility is high, price action is wide and whippy but in the end, settles in the center of the range. As profiles are built they can become somewhat mutated and they never look exactly like the examples shown. The actual patterns are unique but all fall within the three types. You should be able to identify the three types of profiles in your charts with the assistance of the VP tool. You will notice that the profiles may be split and separated within

one trading range; there may be profiles within profiles which create patterns of their own. The following are the three types of variations each of the three main profiles may transform into.

3 Types of Transformations:
1. Double Distribution
2. Positive Skew
3. Negative Skew

A <u>Double Distribution</u> takes the shape of a capital B. The separation between the two profiles is an area of major support or resistance. There is a very high likelihood that once a double distribution is formed price will not return into the original profile a high percentage of the time. In fact, it is so high that I have created a strategy by which the trader can trade away from the prior profile in the event price trades back towards the prior profiles outer limit trading ranges; this is called the double distribution strategy.

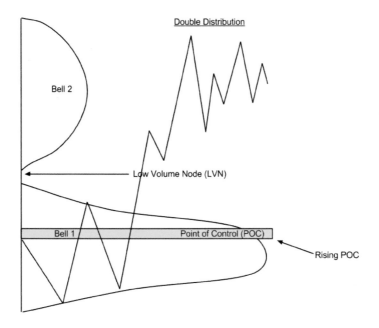

4.2 Double Distribution

In the above image we show a double distribution being formed by the upper profile labeled Bell 2 (Bell Curve 2), the separation is essentially a volume void where little volume has traded at price. This is also known as a low-volume node (LVN). This LVN is the buying area during the next retest.

In the above example price has traded into the upper bell curve, if price were to trade lower down into the LVN, the trader would have the perfect opportunity for a long entry. By combining this selloff into the LVN with a price action buy pattern we have a reliable method for entering an order. This method is known as the **Double Distribution Buy Setup**.

4.3 Price Action Buy Setup

As part of the Double Distribution Buy Setup we look for a selloff into the LVN separator. But before entering a trade we must wait for a price action buy setup to increase the probabilities of success. In 4.3 we see price quickly selling off before stabilizing. The arrow indicates the first buying opportunity which shows price closing above the highs of the prior sideways trading range. This Price Action pattern when found at an important level such as the double distribution is valuable for identifying prime buying opportunities. This indicator which identifies a buy side setup is available at www.FuturesTradeRoom.com and will identify this specific pattern automatically on any time-frame.

If we go back to 4.2 you can see the point of control in the lower profile (Bell 1). This is a rising POC, this will tend to skew the profile to the upside. This means volume (value) is being built higher. It is telling us that there are higher lows built into the price action. A profile can be skewed up or down depending on the development of volume traded at price. As more contracts are traded above the POC, the point of control tends to rise as the profile is skewed to the upside. A skewed upward profile is a solid indication of upward trend bias and lower support levels. It takes commitment of capital to skew a profiles volume in one direction so that it changes the POC. Since buying volume skews bars to the upside I've created a script for identifying directional bias based on this concept; this too is available as part of the FTR Manual Trading System Package.

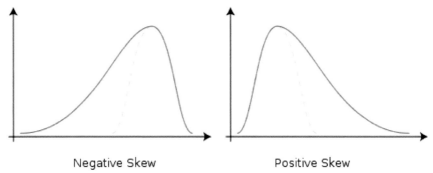

Negative Skew   Positive Skew

4.4 Positive and negative skew.

A positive skew builds value higher, whereas a negative skew builds value lower; the standard deviation levels of the profile becomes skewed as well. The upside of the positive skew profile contains price action that is flat to the upside. You can visualize this as a pattern with higher lows trading up towards a flat top, like an ascending triangle. The negative skew is the opposite, lower highs with a flat bottom, like a descending triangle. In the case of the positive skewed profile, we can expect price to spend less time to the downside and more time to the upside. Buying the lows below VWAP is also an option for a high probability strategy when combined with these concepts. The inverse is true for the negative skew profile as well, less time near the highs and more time spent on the lows. With this knowledge of profile skew we can easily identify the direction of the market based on volume.

The positive skew profile is also known as a buying profile, shaped like a "p", a sell profile shaped like a "b". It can be called a P Profile or a b Profile. The negative skew profile (b) is known as a sell profile. A positive skew (p) indicates that long positions should be taken on major pullbacks.

Having the correct tools to properly identify market opportunities is essential to sustainable profits as a trader. Head over to FuturesTradeRoom.com to download a free copy of the Volume Profile Indicator for NinjaTrader7.

Quiz
Why does buying a double distribution volume void (LVN) level have a high probability of success?

> A.   Price has distributed into a new value area and does not want to trade back into the original value area. The LVN acts as a definitive level separating the top profile from the bottom profile in a double distribution.

SECTION TWO:

DEVELOPMENT

Chapter 5:

Trading Zones

Trading Zones

The Volume Profile represents all the volume data seen on the trader's chart. However, the volume profile may also contain smaller (tradeable) value areas within the main profile. We look to apply the same value area analysis to each profile, or bell curve shown on the chart. By doing this we add additional tradeable areas to the chart for the intraday trader to take advantage of when looking to meet daily tick targets as outlined in the money management schedule.

For best results, we look to highlight bell curves within the main profile that are relative in size to the main value area. The minor bell curves that look like small mountains act as minor areas of hesitation in the chart and often react the same as the largest ones in a fractal manner, we will cover this development further in the development section.

These value area zones act as price magnets, attracting price and keeping it there for sustained periods. When looking at a profile we must have at least two legs of a chart at a minimum. This will show us how price is reacting to existing orders in the prior leg.

Significant changes in volume can represent rejection areas. If you search the profile for the largest percent change in volume you will also notice a rejection, or hesitation in price at such levels. The strength of such hesitation levels depends on how many times price went through and the volume associated with that price level. The more times price goes through the less strength it has in the future, as price continually trades this level it builds value and no longer has precise reaction points, rather it starts to act as an area of hesitation and eventual price deflection as it does not want to trade there any longer (fully developed elongated profile).

Quiz
Why do we analyze at least 2 legs of a swing within the volume profile?

A. To see how price is reacting to open positions in the prior leg.

Chapter 6:

LVN and HVN

LVN and HVN

The Low Volume Node (LVN) and High Volume Node (HVN) make up an important part of the volume profile trading strategy. It is possible to break a profile into multiple minor profiles and have multiple entry points based off the LVN and HVN points.

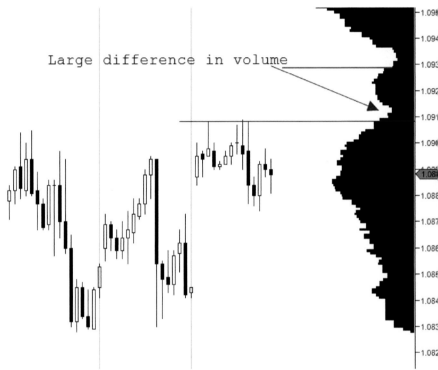

6.1 depicts a large difference in volume at 1.0910, with price being rejected multiple times.

For price to break through this level to the upside, it must pass through quickly on higher volume, any weak attempts to challenge this area will be met with immediate resistance.

Price must pass through quickly if it is to move to the upside because traders that are trapped near the blue line are looking to offset long positions. However, if price quickly goes through the area they will be holding a winning position and will be more likely willing to hold onto it.

This distinct volume void is referred to as a Low Volume Node (LVN), a distinct area where trading interest drops off. An LVN with little to no volume acts as a black hole. This means price will pass through the area very quickly if it is able to make it past the LVN. The LVN areas can also be used as high probability bounce areas for trading if price approaches it with declining momentum. The secret is to understand the way prices are moving into the LVN. In the prior example, the development of the bars is shifted to the downside in a negative skew, they contain long wicks to the upside. This is an indication of low trading interest near the upper volume void (blue line area). A classical volume analysis of the vertical volume would indicate declining volume. However, since there is some volume traded in the void we know that it contains prior orders which may be offset when price comes into that area. In the next screenshot, you will see a large wide range bar on high volume pass through the area with the next bar testing for support and taking off to the upside without looking back.

6.2 showing a wide range bar with price closing above the LVN, then returning briefly to test the top of the LVN before launching to the upside.

This decisive move most likely involves commercial traders, they understand that if price moves very quickly they increase the likelihood of prior long positions holding onto those positions and even adding to those positions as price goes into the green rather than offsetting.

Many strategies can be created by utilizing the LVN areas as trading zones. This we will discuss in detail in the order-flow trading section. I have found great success in utilizing bid/ask order-flow data in conjunction with volume printing at price. For example, if price is approaching the LVN from below with low momentum and volume traded at price starts to build at the ask with price stalling it is usually a good indication of a rejection to the downside. This analysis can be further analyzed by utilizing order-flow footprint technology which will track and print each bid/ask for your review. Such detailed observation involves looking at footprint or time and sales and does involve direct competition with algorithmic programs which compute and trade via patterns found in the order-book. It is recommended that tick charts be used when dialing down to such microscopic levels of analysis. Depending on market liquidity the following Fibonacci based volume or tick sizes can be used in Futures and tend to give good results: 89t, 144t, 233t, 987t.

LVNs can be used for areas of entry as well as areas for stop losses. A stop loss can be put on the other side of an LVN. If price is to cross the LVN there is a good chance that it will eventually continue in that direction therefore a stop loss on the other side of an LVN is it good idea. There is often the case that there is a wall or ledge before an LVN this is shown as a build out in the volume profile just before an LVN. The price action of a chart would look to be flat and severely cut off. It may act as a very strong level of resistance in the future. The depth at which you can utilize a volume profile depends on your experience and background as a trader. If you have a good solid understanding of technical analysis and have spent considerable time in front of the charts outlining patterns and backtesting you will be able to refer to the profile as confirmation of your trade ideas.

The problem with most traders introduced into volume profile trading is that they look to trade the profile itself and not the chart. They understand the basics of how price moves around the volume profile, but they don't know whether to buy, sell, or do nothing. The profile alone cannot always tell you this, it must be combined with another method of analysis; however, it is very robust and can be used with almost any method, even trend lines or channels.

6.3 Ledge before an LVN on the right, with price action showing extreme rejection on the left.

This area in 6.3 will contain many trapped buyers acting as a clean area of resistance in the future. The underlying market conditions should be bearish for a short position at this LVN ledge. If price shows activity outside of the LVN this is initiating activity which would mean continuation through the LVN. A low volume approach to an LVN at a changing volume profile level is a clear sign of rejection. The ability to know the difference is what separates a high probability trader from a gambler. The recognition of such patterns can only be understood by close study of real market examples out on the charts in real time. I recommend as part of your studies that you load up a chart for each section and identify on the charts multiple examples of the topics covered. We learn best by repetition so don't be afraid to backtest on a regular basis. During the weekend I will often run the market replay tool in NinjaTrader and practice trading in fast forward. By doing this you will increase the rate at which you learn, you will also begin to see how holding onto trades longer than you are used to can help with building your profitability. Download a platform such as NinjaTrader and learn to utilize the Market Replay tool as an invaluable asset to your training.

A few definitions and key points to review before moving on:

Ledge/Wall: A distinct separation in volume.

Trap: Is a price level with high volume, usually at or near a distinguished low volume node where the majority of traders are in anticipation of an imminent price move in the other direction. The high-volume node next to the low volume node shows an abundance of traders trapped in that area. This will act as future support or resistance.

HVN: A HVN represents an increased level of interest at price. If the HVN is not followed by a LVN it is not a distinct area of rejection, rather it is a temporary short-term rejection point such as a swing or pivot shown on the price action, the HVN is often taken out on future price tests.

When you're getting into a position it is best to have identified area for your stop loss, if you are not using a specific system which identifies your stop loss location you should be putting your stops on the other side of an LVN. If there are no such distinguished stop loss levels, you should let the trade go.

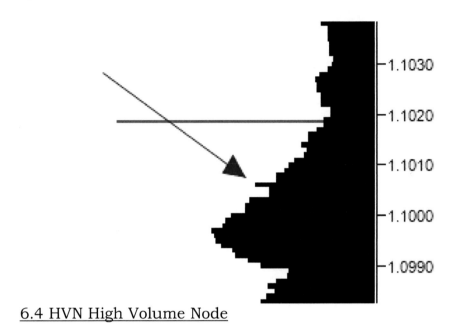

6.4 HVN High Volume Node

Why does price need above average volume to break through an LVN?

A. Because historically that level has acted as a delineation point and price cannot pass through without new initiative trading activity (new buyers).

Chapter 7:

Profile Acceptance

Once we've identified the tradable profiles we can look to see how price approaches the profile in order to set up our trade direction bias.

This process occurs as follows:
Initial Bounce, Probe, Retest, Reject, Distribute.

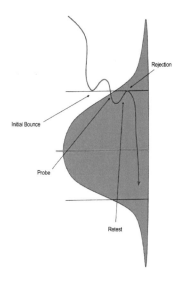

7.1 Initial bounce, probe, retest, reject and distribute
In the above example the Market is coming from the upside approaching the 2 StdDev value area high. Price initially bounces higher before returning to probe into the value area, it quickly reverses to retest the bounce area before going into one of the two phases of price action.

Price can either reject off this level or be magnetized to it. Price will often become magnetized if trading activity slows down and the move loses momentum. In this case price is quickly rejected and continues downward to distribute and test the unfair lows on the other side of the profile.

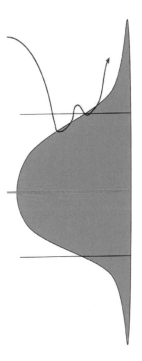

7.2 Support at 2 StdDev Value Area High.
In 7.2 the Market approaches the profile from above attempting to probe but finding support at the 2StdDev value area, price exits the value area and on a retest bounces to the upside. Sustained trading time above this area with volume constitutes support. Price no longer wishes to trade the lower profile. Any deep short-term tests of the profile should be met with highly aggressive buying activity.

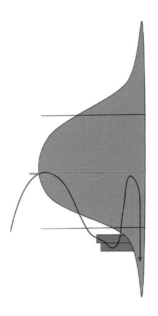

7.3 POC Resistance to old volume

The Market tests the Highest Volume Traded (POC) and is immediately rejected before coming down to the unfair lows. At the unfair lows buyers step in to bring price up, they leave an HVN support bar behind as price continues back into the prior rejected POC. This HVN leaves us a clue that there has been a lot of trading interest in this area. This area will act as a futures pain point for long traders if price falls below this level. It is also clear that price is not willing to trade in the POC area as it is usually swiftly rejected. A rejection of the POC on a retest is a clear sign that value is overstated and a probe to the downside is imminent. Since the HVN consists of relatively new orders we can expect a breakdown of this level as traders who were long exit degrading positions thereby creating additional sell orders. Any retests of this HVN from a downside retest will be met with much resistance as losing long positions offset orders near break even.

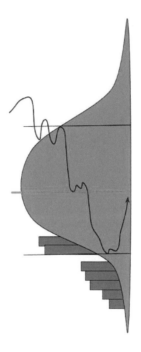

7.4
The Market enters the profile from above, passes through the value area to the value area low and is rejected at the LVN in conjunction with a 2StdDev level. Price is contained within the value area eventually returning to the POC if it has not enough volume participation to go anywhere else.

The Market clearly made a very large move and is likely overextended, it probed into the profile and quickly passes to the unfair lows where it tests the LVN. It is on this test that the astute trader looks to enter longs with stops on the other side of the LVN, after such a large extensive move price may look to return to the POC as traders await new information.

As price tests important profile levels, significant changes in order-flow data can tell us if the buyers, or the sellers are likely to prevail.
After the probe price will come back to the profile value area high to retest.

Bid X Ask footprint data can give clues to the market participants aggregated intention.

If on the retest of the VAH, the order-flow delta turns negative, it is likely that sellers are loading up at this level and so we now expect lower prices to come.

Rather than invest tens of thousands into overly complex order-flow platforms, I've created a bare bones essentials only order-flow package for NinjaTrader7. These order-flow indicators allow you the ability to see at a glance if the buyers, or sellers are in control.

What is the price action procedure for approaching a developed profile?

A.   Initial Bounce, Probe, Retest, Reject and Distribute.

Chapter 8:

PROFILE DEVELOPMENT

The Development of Profiles

As a profile develops it can be skewed up or down, if a profile is skewed to the upside value is said to be building higher. The price action on the chart should show long tails to the downside which indicate conviction of buyers. This indicates less time the market spends trading at lower levels. Less trading at such levels indicates lower acceptance of those price levels. Think of an uppercase P, this is the shape of a buying profile. A profile shaped like a lowercase b shows the volume development to the downside, which is indicative of a sell profile.

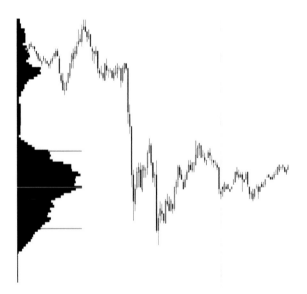

8.1"b" profile showing downward development.

8.2 "P" profile showing upward volume development

A profile developing to the upside (P Profile) is leaving a trail of short traders holding onto losing positions. As price returns to test the lows of development those traders will offset positions (buyback) thereby causing price to continue upwards in the case of a "P" profile. The P profile consists of higher lows. Once price has moved significantly enough and an upward trend has been identified, price may look to shake out long traders by dumping to test the swing lows and take out stop losses. This is usually a bullish play. This is a common strategy of algos that see price is overall moving higher and want to run stops to accumulate and quickly bring price up to new high. Please know that they *don't* want to bring

you along for the ride. If you exit your long position,
it   allows   them   to

accumulate more longs before price launches and continues higher. This is smart money (real smart), knowing price is going higher overall and buying the big dip. We call this the stop flush or stop sweep. This is a great buying strategy to get the best fills.

To assist in the identification of the current volume based trend, the volume profile indicator has been uploaded to www.FuturesTradeRoom.com, it is the same one used in this book and is available for NinjaTrader7.

Where should you be buying in a P profile?

> A.   Any short-term dips below major lows (stop sweeps).
>
> If the bar does not close below the prior low and stay there for a substantial amount of time it is considered a test and the trade is still valid. Often such a dip to the downside is the best "Buy Low Sell High" type of entry. Be sure to take into the account the potential for price action to sell off even further before rebounding. Proper position sizing is essential to allow you to sit through the increased volatility at these extreme and often questionable levels.

SECTION THREE:

ORDER-FLOW

Chapter 9:

TIME AND SALES

Time and Sales

Before we get into using order-flow trading as a tool for reading the details behind a profile it would help to understand the T&S.

Time and Sales is available on every platform.

For liquid markets I am only interested in the sales which show the price and size of the order, at the bid or ask.

Assuming there is a spread between the Bid and Ask;

To be a buyer at market you will get filled at the Ask.

To be a seller at market you will get filled at the Bid.

Occasionally the BidxAsk will be at the same price and this usually occurs in fast markets.

To get an ideal buy you would Buy Bid.

To get an ideal sell you would sell Ask.

Based on some studies on order-flow I have found that for every order found in the Level 2 order-book (pending orders) there are multiples of at market orders. Above Ask is considered aggressive buyers and Below Bid considered Aggressive Sellers. This will be sufficient for our purposes in analyzing T&S data.

Today's trading software has allowed the big players to hide their orders. A 100 lot or 1000 lot trader can now get filled through default platform algorithms that will randomize the total amount of orders into a string of smaller orders under 10 contracts. Or it can show up as a string of random numbers in the T&S. Dropping large orders into the market is essentially showing your hand. If you are a long-term trader it might not matter, but if you are scalping it will not only affect your fill price, but your entry price range will be a target for predatory traders looking to trade against you in hopes of catching the landslide that will occur during your liquidation.

The T&S can be used to show interest at the current moment in time relative to where price is within any patterns on the chart.

The raw T&S data can be overwhelming because executed orders of many sizes are quickly passing through. I ignore most of orders that come through the T&S. I'm concerned about large orders, or if the speed of transactions picks up. This will draw my attention to that market to look for opportunity.

Any further analysis of the raw T&S data requires the use of some data logging tools. These tools will represent the data in a way that the trader can use to identify patterns in the order-flow. A tool I use for learning about market data is a statistical analysis platform, R Studio. R allows the trader to load price and size data for a market and run statistical tests to learn about patterns in the data. Furthermore, this data can then be fed into machine learning AI algorithms to further enhance the ability of the trader to learn what works when it comes to beating the market.

The Volume Profile works by extracting the T&S data and records it on the chart. When an order comes into the market at a specific price, the volume profile adds those order to the horizontal histogram. This horizontal line can be seen being built in real-time if the indicator is set to "calculate on bar close = false". The volume profile also visually represents the T&S data as a bell curve with understandable patterns that the trader can use to strategically devise trade direction and specific entry opportunities.

In the past I've been able to use the volume profile in conjunction with price action and volume spread analysis patterns to predict price moves worth tens of thousands of dollars per contract. When you can allow position sizing to work in your favor so that you can allow your trade the room to fluctuate for some time before the real move happens you'll see that the volume profile really is the crystal ball of any and every market out there.

Q. What can the T&S plot in its entirety?

A. Best Bid, Best Ask, Last Sale, Timestamp, Order Size, if the order was a Block Order.

Chapter 10:

VOLUME DELTA

FOOTPRINT

Volume Delta FootPrint

A footprint chart logs the T&S data into columns like so.

[BID X ASK]

The left side contains orders executed at the bid (Sellers) and the right side contains orders executed at the Ask (Buyers).

[MARKET SELLERS X MARKET BUYERS]

Delta is the "change in", or the difference. Volume Delta simply tracks the difference between the Buyers and the Sellers.

There are two types of Volume Delta tracking methods:

1. Cumulative Volume Delta – tracks the change for the current session. As each bar is generated, it saves the data and shows the running total as above or below zero. Cumulative delta can be used to identify the current overall trend, or to see who is in control of the current trend. If buyers are in control because of a strong positive delta, we would expect price to continue higher. If for example a sudden drop below an important level is met with resistance, followed by a failed retest of that area, it is possible that price could collapse very quickly since all the longs which have accumulated made panic and unload at once.

2. Current Bar Volume Delta – tracks the delta for the current bar, once a` new bar is formed it will reset the count to zero and start recording delta for the new bar. The current bar delta should be watched as price is fluctuating near important price levels.

I'll take you through the steps for analyzing delta and footprint for scalping.

First decide on a timeframe, a lower timeframe will allow you to sit and watch as each bar, along with order information is populated. I prefer to use either a 3minute or 144tick timeframe. This way the chart flows horizontally rather than vertically. I want to be able to see the [Bid x Ask] prints as it approaches the unfair highs and unfair lows of a profile. The amount of volume participation at these levels gives me clues as to how well price is moving, and how much interest it has at such important levels that other traders have been anticipating.

For instance, let's assume a P Profile with a price action buy setup is being formed:

Price is forming a P profile with volume (value) trading higher. Price briefly dips to the swing low which also is an LVN and takes out the low by 3 ticks...
At this point I am looking at the volume delta and footprint. I want to see the at-market sellers at the bid decline (left column) and the at-market buyers (right column) at the ask increase. This shows me the right time to get in. If price dips through the low on high selling volume, get out. If other buyers step

in once price ticks higher, hold on because there is a good chance price will return to the prior highs.

Another option is rather than looking at the bid/ask I look at the change between the bid and ask, or the delta. This gives me just one positive or negative number. It shows if there are more buyers or sellers; by doing this I can ignore the T&S, ignore the footprint and just watch delta increase or decrease at the unfair value areas highs/lows.

Broad view -> Cumulative Delta
Narrow view -> Current Bar Delta
Inspection view -> Delta
Microscopic view -> FootPrint

Chapter 11:

COMMITMENT OF TRADERS

The COT

The COT (Commitment of Traders) can be found in the footprint chart. It is the value with the highest amount of committed contacts at price. This price is highlighted and acts as the value areas for the footprints column.When the COT is in the middle of the bar it is indecisive. When at the extremes it shows intent to move price higher or lower.

121*255
111*299
300*422
141*131
124*145

A COT can create something call an Opening when it occurs at the highs or lows.
An opening is when the COT prints at the high of a bar but price backs off and trades lower without coming back immediately. This area contains many trapped buyers and sellers. Price will often return to this area to pass through the opening.

300*422
121*255
111*299
141*131
124*145

A COT can also create something called a Cap.
A cap is similar to an opening in how it is created, however a cap concludes an auction. There is a decisive end to a move as the buyers cease to buy anymore.

A cap at the high of a move with look like this:
300*0
178*115
121*325
When a Cap or an Opening occurs near the unfair value area high/low it is a clue as to whether price is going to return to that level (opening) or not come back (capped).

SECTION FOUR:

··

BECOMING
PROFITABLE

··

Chapter 12:

PSYCHOLOGY OF TRADING

Psychology of Trading

In the face of a perceived threat our sympathetic nervous system activates physiological changes in the body. This generally happens on a subconscious level. This means that when the reptilian brain perceives a threat it kicks on the switch which triggers a chemical reaction in your body which automatically puts you in fight or flight state. This state of heightened awareness can make you quick to react. Although you are safe at your trade station and know you are not in any life or death situation, your brain may be perceiving the losing position as a threat, your ability to make rational decisions are limited at this point. The amygdala perceives the losing position to be a threat to your lifestyle. This is because of built in associations with money. Today we generally need money to maintain the high-status lifestyle we are used to. If you are taking trading seriously you are putting in extensive time, money and energy; all of which are generally finite resources. To lose a trade is to trade not only your capital but also your energy and time associated with that trade. This translates into a level of stress; enough stress and you trigger the fight or flight response. The trader no longer sees the original reason for getting into the trade, he now thinks in terms of fear and greed. When these emotions enter the picture perhaps the trader begins over-trading or attempts to get larger in size to make back losses right away. This never ends well and always exacerbates losses.

Although you may react differently, for the most part it's important to take note of changes in trading behavior due to your current psychological outlook.

Now for the solution.

To trade well you must begin to eliminate the ego. Trading by the seat of your pants offers great opportunity for the ego to show how great it is and how it knew exactly what the market would do, at the exact right time; gratifying the ego through an immediate dopamine hit for being right. Pretty soon, being right is more important than making money, and the trader can end up rewiring their brain to from bad habits. What fires together wires together, don't get caught up in ego trading.

Another problem of ego trading is that when you trade by the seat of your pants you are at the whim of your emotions. A trader under the influence of such physiological stress response can easily trade his account into a deep hole very quickly.

A trader has two tasks, the first is to identify high probability patterns, the second is to execute orders to take advantage of those patterns. Traders wishing to trade for a living must have checklists and systems in place to narrow down specific trade setups which will be executed and monitored according to a specific trade plan.

You will need the following to trade objectively.

1. A robust trade identification method.
2. Repeatable system and checklist for scanning, entering and managing trades.
3. Pre-defined fail safe in place for unpredictable events.

We will briefly unpack these three items. You will want to take out a sheet of paper and create a worksheet that fits you. Remember, if it's not on paper it doesn't exist. Your plan should be made as if it were to be handed off to a trader on your staff which is trading your personal capital. It needs to be easily understood in plain language and with no room for alteration or justification.

A Robust Trade Identification Method

The general purpose of this book was to arm you with a trade identification method for understanding when the market is balanced, or imbalanced. The market goes from balance (consolidation) to imbalance (trending). The volume profile along with the 3 types of profiles clearly show what stage the market is in for your current timeframe.

Once you have come up with a directional bias for the contracts to trade it is time to go through your checklist.

Checklist

The checklist should be like that of a pilot. When flying an aircraft at night or through thick clouds you'd want the assistance of your instruments to guide you. Those instruments are the indicators you choose to use. I personally only rely on leading indicators such as volume, anything else is a derivative of price and is therefore lagging. A volume imbalance is what causes price to move, therefore it is leading price.

My checklist for swing trading involves the following:

A. Timing
Will the trade move in my direction within 3 days?
B. Risk to Reward
Is there sufficient room for the trade to develop, or is it already extended and likely to retrace?

C. Economic and Geopolitical Events
Is the market awaiting new information, or is there a news event that could make the trade no longer valid?

D. Are the higher up timeframes supportive of my lower time-frame directional bias? Are they in consolidation or trend? This will have a direct effect on the quality of the trend.

Failsafe
A failsafe mechanism is designed to activate when all goes wrong. The purpose is to limit damages and return to a safe condition.
My failsafe is to immediately neutralize positions to mitigate unforeseen risk. This can be done by desktop, laptop, cellphone or a phone call to a broker. I have my broker's number written down and have cell phone numbers for the trade desk staff. I also have multiple accounts in the event I need to hedge an order that is stuck in the system.
More important than this is the process by which you decide when to implement the failsafe mechanism.
The process by which you define your plan will depend on your risk tolerance. The idea is that certain markets will only move a certain amount in a given period. If you are scalping for a few ticks then your room for error is virtually nonexistent, you must

execute your failsafe immediately. If your time period is trading the daily chart then you have more time to react.

I generally immediately close out unwanted positions that may have been entered by fatfinger error regardless of PnL. I want to be in control of my account and will not allow a random trade to fit into my trading plan.

The failsafe rules should follow a simple If Then syntax.

For example:
If {emergency event takes place}
Then {flatten all positions}

Having an objective set of rules to follow will help you maintain consistency of the equity curve over a long period of time. When you become an order enterer - entering orders as described by the trading system, you eliminate subjectivity and emotional influences from your decision-making process.

Your plan should be a living document, when you find something that repeats and should be corrected, update your plan to represent this discovery and implement it accordingly. Be sure to wait until after the end of the trading day to recreate the plan. You will then execute the new plan the next day, never deviate from the plan during the current trading session! That's called justifying your irrational behavior!

If you believe you have discovered a flaw in your system, or you begin to ignore your rules stop trading for the day. Research, reflect and confirm your ideas before getting back to the charts. Leaving this much time between your plan modifications will ensure you are not revenge trading.

Chapter 13:

POSITION MANAGEMENT

When to hold and when to fold

How you manage your positions can mean the difference between locking in gains or taking unnecessary losses. Two traders can take the same trade and have totally different outcomes, it all comes down to your ability to manage the trade into a profitable one.

To make this work you're going to need to reverse engineer the way you manage your trades starting with the formula for positive expectancy.

Formula for Positive Expectancy

Expectancy = (%Win x Avg. Winner) - (%Loss x Avg. Loser)

I.E.

A strategy that wins $1500, 60% of the time, and loses $300, 40% of the time.

(60% x 1500) - (40% x 300)

$780 = 900 – 120

This system has a positive expectancy of $780. This means that if you stick to the plan and stay consistent you are expected to profit over the long haul.

This is where automating your strategy comes into play. It relieves the trader of missing trades that meet setup parameters, thereby increasing trade frequency and allowing the laws of probabilities to work themselves out.

Formula for Negative Expectancy:
System wins $100, 90% of the time, and loses $900, 10% of the time.

(90% x 100) - (10% x 900)

$0 = 90-90

Although this system appears good on paper because it produces long winning streaks, all the gains disappear after a few losses. This system creates zero expectancy of profit over a long-time period. Factor in commissions and you have yourself a guaranteed losing system.

I hope you've been saving your trade data because it is truly valuable. Go take a look at your trade history and performance report to see what your numbers look like. Put them into the formula and see if you have a positive or negative expectancy of success. You can use this method to tweak your open position handling methods.

Perhaps you only win about 35% of the time, that means your winners are a lot larger than your losers if you are to be successful.

If on the other hand you win about 70% of the time you can afford to have winners close to the size of your losers.

For many trading I am for +70% with winners 3 times the size of the losers or greater.

With automation you can be wildly successful with +50% win rate and winners 2 times larger than your losers.

I personally have found that I get the best results when I close a trade that is fluctuating near breakeven and stagnating. This means the momentum has been sucked out of the trade and new participation is required for it to move. If no new players come into the market, then the existing ones will begin to liquidate. My best trades are those that generally work out right away. This is not enough however, I must allow those positive trades time to develop into a trend. If the momentum dries up the bars will begin to overlap, and the profile begins to build. If the market starts ranging wide and whippy I'll close the position and get out. If it consolidates in a tight range, I'll stay in and bring stops in to lock some profit. If the market still goes nowhere I'll really tighten the stops up, or if I notice a few of my other positions are also stagnate I'll flatten everything and wait until a new setup is created.

This is important, once you exit a trade you must wait for a new setup to be created. This takes time, depending on your time frame; for intraday traders this could be a few hours, for daily chart traders this could be a week or more.

For instance, at the time of writing this I have not been able to enter into a Crude Oil trade for the past month because I have not received any signals which matched my trading strategies based on volume profile development in the Daily time frame. The market has moved around a bit, but I will stay out of the market because I will only trade the patterns which are aligned with my trading plan and strategy.

Do this and you will be rewarded with trades that succeed and perform like how it did in back-testing mode.

Sure, you'll sit idle while the market fluctuates, but you'll be safe while others take unnecessary losses.

Chapter 14:

TECHNICAL ANALYSIS

Technical Analysis

Trading the Volume Profile would not be complete without a throughout understanding of Technical Analysis. Technical Analysis is the study of the aggregate psychology of all market participants. The market participants are influenced by common perceptions and this leads to a group think which creates recognizable patterns. These patterns are self-reinforcing in that traders looking for the patterns and will trade into the completion of such patterns. However, this is not always the case, a sharp liquidation at a key level could put a crack in the foundation of a pattern and cause it to collapse under its own weight as traders scramble to exit.

To make the best use of the Volume Profile we want to combine technical patterns with the profile to identify imbalances in the market; *it is these imbalances that cause the market to move quickly in one direction.* Once the market moves quickly in one direction it attracts the attention of other speculative traders which act as a self-reinforcing mechanism for price to continue. At market imbalance areas it can be useful to follow time and sales data in search of Block Trades which indicate institutional, or commercial participation at such imbalance levels. Large trader participation at imbalance level can push price over the edge and start a new trend.

The ABCD Extension

Pattern formations often shapeshift. They can take morph into noise, or they can take the form of opposing patterns, signaling indecision. The important takeaway is to look for what the formation is trying to achieve. An ABCD extension may not always look like a textbook example, in fact if I see a textbook style formation I tend to worry that it will fail under its own anticipation. However, it appears that there are enough traders not in the know about such patterns to warrant the of trading such blatantly obvious patterns which have taken months to form.

To get the most out of pattern trading I am looking for the way the volume is developing in the formation, this shows me the intention of the traders involved.

However, what's most important to me is the imbalance. Understanding where trades are profitable or unprofitable gives the clues behind the validity   of   setup.

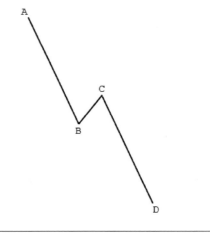

ABCD Extension Pattern

Here is an example of a real time ABCD extension I am considering shorting in CC at the time of writing.

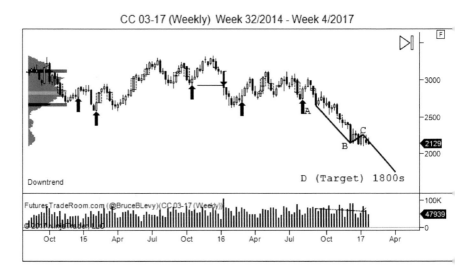

CC 03-17 (Weekly) Week 32/2014 - Week 4/2017

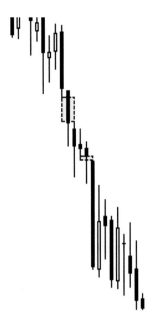

Closeup of the Weekly Bear ABCD Pattern in Cocoa

Notice the coil and how volume is developing to the lower portion of the coil. It is ready to bust through the bottom as longs liquidation in fear.

The Ascending Triangle

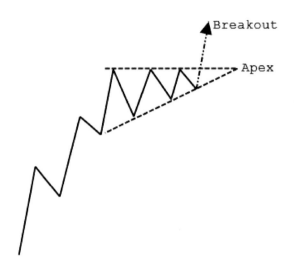

A Bullish Ascending Triangle formation shown here in the African Rand Weekly Chart.

The pattern is characterized as having higher lows with a flat top. The breakout should occur at approximately 3/4 of the apex of the pattern. The apex is where the ascending lower trendline meets the flat top.

It is good that volume is declining, as seen by the linear regression line overlaid onto the volume panel.

Bear Wedge

CL 03-17 (Monthly) 1/2011 - 1/2017

The Bear Wedge appears like the Ascending Triangle in that it has a rising bottom. However, the main difference is that the prior trend is down and it can have a flat to slightly ascending top. The following diagram will illustrate this.

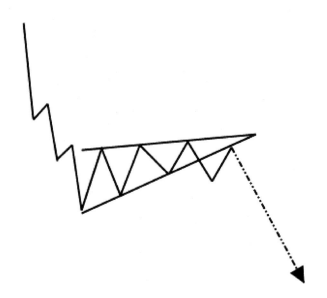

The Bear Wedge comes in after a downtrend as traders take profits and attempt to accumulate, however volume often dries up and the pattern fails. Once the prior swing lows are taken out and the trendline violated, traders liquidate long positions and sellers begin to come in. The pattern has an extension of the length of the prior downleg. Notice that I refer to longs liquidating and new sellers coming in. This combination leads to quick movements that are hard to gain back. If we can get into these positions before this happens we are often in good shape has price will have a very hard time getting back up right away. The prior swing lows that were built along the bull trendline will now act as overhead resistance as traders offset losing position to get back to breakeven on their positions and avoid larger losses.

While writing this I have taken a short break to focus on trading. Since I apply what I teach here to my trading I have the following Cocoa chart showing how price passed through the bottom side of the formation, retraced, found resistance before dramatically selling off nearly as described many weeks before. Notice how the Weekly Cocoa chart in the Bearish ABCD section holds a bearish wedge in the daily timeframe as well. This bearish pattern within a larger pattern is additional confirmation that both timeframes are trading in the same direction.

Bull Flag

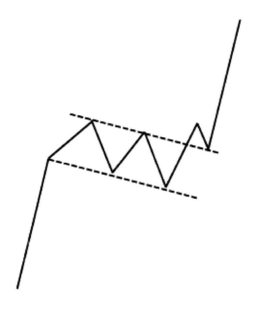

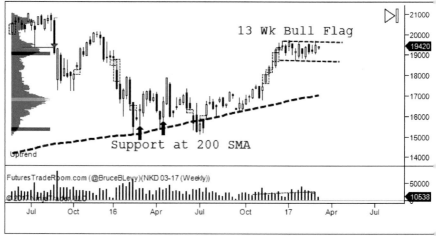

The bullflag is indicative of accumulation being built into the consolidation. It is merely a sign of the setup resting before continuing higher.

A bullflag can be measured by adding the upleg, or flagpole of the pattern to the top of the consolidation channel.

Another more modest option is to double the height of the consolidation pattern.

As you can see in the image above the NKD Weekly has found support near the 200 Day SMA and broke out higher just shy of the Oct/Nov highs. During this phase it is wise to buy the lows and hold for the breakout. Once price closes outside of the prior consolidation channel those traders that are short will start to liquidate and cause price to find support at the breakout level.

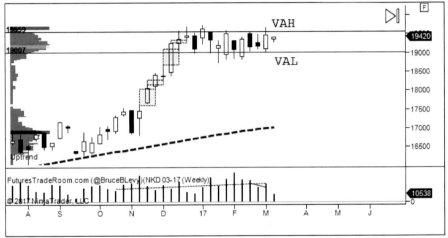

NKD 03-17 (Weekly) Week 29/2016 - Week 10/2017

When I first learned Technical Analysis I was shown ideal setups that were already completed, and they were all successful. The problem was during real time charting the formations are not complete yet and we don't know if they are going to succeed or not. For best results you'll want to head out onto the charts and identify these setups in progress. Use your experience to judge if it is trade worthy.

If you are interested in position or swing trading you'll want to use the chart drawing tool to outline these patterns. The learning process is much more effective, and you'll have much more confidence if you watch as the long-term chart develops on a consistent basis.

Chapter 15:

CONTEXTUAL TRADING

Chapter 15

Contextual Trading

Contextual trading involves combining the volume profile, technical analysis and multiple time frames to read the markets overall development. In the following charts we will look for clues as to what the chart is telling us.

Rather than trying to predict what the next bar will do we will focus on predicting the scenarios by which price will develop.

6M 03-17 (Daily) 10/19/2016 - 1/19/2017

6M 03-17 (Daily) - Before

The Peso sold off hard in early November during the surprise Trump election win. The large downbar closed below the prior trading range and traded sideways until the 2017 New Year before breaking out of the range and closing below the two month consolidation zone.

During early January price held the level as Mean Reversion buyers attempted to accumulate. Notice this area does not represent any type of bearish continuation pattern.

Based on your analysis what scenario do you think will take place next?

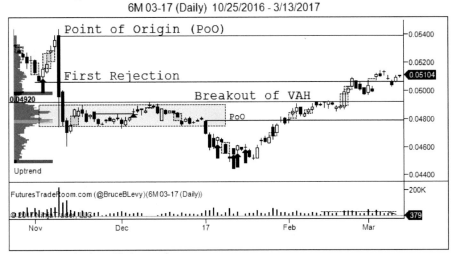

6M 03-17 (Daily) 10/25/2016 - 3/13/2017

6M 03-17 (Daily) - After

The centerline of the consolidation channel acts as a reversal point. If price is able to get above this level it is likely to reverse the polarity of the trend.

In this case we use a concept called the Point of Origin, or PoO for short. This Point of Origin may also be used a more accurate location. I always prefer to use specific levels of meaning rather than arbitrary figures.

If you look closely price gaps above the lower PoO line, trades sideways and finds some resistance at the VAH prior to breaking out.

The next level is the First Rejection. This area is a prior swing low, price will often come to a pivot level like this to the tick before being rejected; notice how erratic and undefined the volume profile is - this is a sign that price is likely to fill in the area as long as the current uptrend persists.

So seeing where we are now on the chart we can expect price to target the next higher PoO level from the November election. This would be inline with the overall uptrend. I must emphasis that we don't want to trade against this trend.

What is the PoO exactly?

The PoO is the Opening price of the bar that closed outside of the prior trend or trading range. These areas are important inflection points, acting as support, resistance and targets.

Be sure to apply what you've learned on the charts by backtesting over many years of historical data to get the most out of this book and eventually you'll begin to have confidence in understanding how markets operate through direct observation.